ALICE IN WONDERLAND

Dramatized
by
Charlotte B. Chorpenning

Based upon the book
by
Lewis Carroll

The Dramatic Publishing Company
Woodstock, Illinois • London, England • Melbourne, Australia

*** NOTICE ***

The amateur and stock acting rights to this work are controlled exclusively by THE DRAMATIC PUBLISHING COMPANY without whose permission in writing no performance of it may be given. Royalty fees are given in our current catalogue and are subject to change without notice. Royalty must be paid every time a play is performed whether or not it is presented for profit and whether or not admission is charged. A play is performed anytime it is acted before an audience. All inquiries concerning amateur and stock rights should be addressed to: THE DRAMATIC PUBLISHING COMPANY, 311 Washington St., Woodstock, Illinois 60098.

COPYRIGHT LAW GIVES THE AUTHOR OR HIS AGENT THE EXCLUSIVE RIGHT TO MAKE COPIES.

This law provides authors with a fair return for their creative efforts. Authors earn their living from the royalties they receive from book sales and from the performance of their work. Conscientious observance of copyright law is not only ethical, it encourages authors to continue their creative work. This work is fully protected by copyright. No alterations, deletions or substitutions may be made in the work without the prior written consent of the publisher. No part of this work may be reproduced or transmitted in any form or by any means, electronic or mechanical, including photocopy, recording, videotape, film, or any information storage and retrieval system, without permission in writing from the publisher. It may not be performed either by professionals or amateurs without payment of royalty. All rights, including but not limited to the professional, motion picture, radio, television, videotape, foreign language, tabloid, recitation, lecturing, publication, and reading are reserved. On all programs this notice should appear: "Produced by special arrangement with THE DRAMATIC PUBLISHING COMPANY of Woodstock, Illinois."

(ALICE IN WONDERLAND)

ISBN 0-87129-035-9

ALICE IN WONDERLAND

A Play in Three Acts
For Eighteen Characters And Extras

CHARACTERS

WHITE RABBIT
ALICE
CATERPILLAR
DUCHESS
COOK
FROG-FOOTMAN
MARCH HARE
MAD HATTER
DORMOUSE
MOCK TURTLE
GRYPHON
TWEEDLEDUM
TWEEDLEDEE
KING OF HEARTS
KNAVE OF HEARTS
RED QUEEN
WHITE QUEEN
EXECUTIONER

PLACE: Wonderland.

TIME: Wonderland is timeless.

NOTE: The play may be given on a curtained stage, or against any very simple background. Directions for the making of some of the necessary props are at the end of the play. Costumes should follow the Tenniel illustrations, and as often as possible the stage pictures should include the pictures in the book—e.g., the familiar one showing the HATTER and the MARCH HARE leaning elbows on the DORMOUSE, etc.

WHAT PEOPLE ARE SAYING about *Alice in Wonderland...*

"This is the best Alice play I've ever seen. We have produced it twice now (10 years apart), the first one was my favorite performance until the second one blew it out of the water! Great for character development and multiple spotlights. Everybody has a chance for a best performance!"

Peg Ginsberg,
Mt. Horeb High School,
Mt. Horeb, Wis.

"I chose *Alice in Wonderland* as the very first play at our school so that any student who wanted to be involved could be. It was easy to expand for extra actors. It is a show that students can add their own touches to."

Christine Hopper,
Frances Harper Junior High,
Davis, Calif.

"Fast moving, crisp dialogue, colorful characters, workable set—and excellent production. We will do it again and again!"

Anne Stumhofer,
Family Theatre,
Columbus, Ga.

ACT ONE

SCENE: *A curtained stage, empty, except for a definite shaft of light coming obliquely from above, and striking the floor out of sight, offstage.*

AT RISE OF CURTAIN: *The WHITE RABBIT hurries on with a high leap, fanning himself rapidly. He stops, takes a watch from his waistcoat pocket, holds it in the shaft of light, and shakes his head.*

RABBIT. Oh, dear, oh, dear! The Duchess! I shall be late! *(A little scream from above startles the RABBIT.)*

ALICE *(offstage, excited, not afraid)*. Oh! O-h-h-h-h! *(The RABBIT simply indicates ALICE's progress by looking up to the top of the beam of light, and then progressing lower as ALICE's lines follow.)*

RABBIT. Oh, my ears and whiskers! Something has fallen into my rabbit hole!

ALICE *(still offstage)*. Oh! O-h-h-h-h!

RABBIT. It sounds like a little girl.

ALICE *(still offstage)*. Down, down, down! I wonder where I'm falling to?

RABBIT. It talks. It *is* a little girl.

ALICE *(still offstage)*. After such a fall as this I shall think nothing of falling downstairs. I shouldn't say a word even if I fell off the top of a house.

RABBIT *(nodding)*. Which is very likely true.

ALICE *(still offstage)*. How dark it looks ahead!

RABBIT *(fanning himself violently)*. Oh, my fur and fore-paws! She's coming to the edge! What if she should break to bits when she falls off!

ALICE *(still offstage)*. Hi-i-i-i-i! Here I go! *(There is a great thump, and then silence.)*

RABBIT *(listening, "frozen")*. I'm afraid to look. Little girls can't leap like rabbits. *(He starts to see what has happened, terrified of what he will, and fans himself furiously.)* Dear me! Oh, dear me—

(The RABBIT stops, amazed, as ALICE enters, brushing the dust from her apron daintily, perfectly placid, and full of interest.)

ALICE *(curtseying)*. Is this the end?

RABBIT. The question is: Is there any such thing?

ALICE. Of course there is. Everything comes to an end sometime.

RABBIT. It might be a beginning, you know.

ALICE. Beginning of what?

RABBIT. How can I tell till I know more about you? The fall didn't hurt you at all?

ALICE. That it didn't. And it's very curious, because it lasted a very long time.

RABBIT *(nodding to himself)*. That's because you belong here.

ALICE. Where am I?

RABBIT. That all depends on what's going on inside you.

ALICE. I wish you wouldn't talk nonsense.

RABBIT. I wish you'd mind your manners.

ALICE. I didn't mean to be rude.

RABBIT. Then don't be. It doesn't work down here.

ALICE. I only asked: Where am I?

RABBIT. And I told you. You're where you belong. And that depends on what goes on inside of you.

ALICE. I don't know what you mean.

RABBIT. How do you suppose you got down my rabbit hole?

ALICE. I fell. I was sitting by my sister on the river bank and I saw you run by. You were talking to yourself! And then you took a watch out of your pocket and looked at it, and that made me so curious I ran after you. And when you popped down a rabbit hole, I just popped down after you.

RABBIT. And you entirely forgot that little girls can't go down rabbit holes?

ALICE. Why, yes. I just felt inside of me that I *had* to see what you were doing.

RABBIT. Exactly. And so here you are. And you never once stopped to think how in the world you were going to get out again.

ALICE *(alarmed)*. Oh, dear—I think I'll just go back, please. Back where I came from.

RABBIT. It's one thing to think so and another to do it.

ALICE. I wish you wouldn't contradict me all the time!

RABBIT. Oh, very well! Go right ahead and fall up again.

ALICE. You don't fall up. You climb. *(The RABBIT fans himself, tapping his foot and smiling at ALICE significantly.)* Where I fell off—it went up like a wall. Suppose I couldn't climb it?

RABBIT. I am supposing it.

ALICE. It's a little frightening. Oh, Rabbit, please, I want to go back!

RABBIT. It's no use whatever to want that.

ALICE. Why not?

RABBIT. Every hour is a one-way road. It will take you wherever you choose, but it will never take you back again.

ALICE. I want to see the sky! I want to see my kitten. *(The RABBIT fans himself faster, smiling.)* Isn't there any way to get out of here?

RABBIT. Dozens of ways. *(He recites.)*

There's a way for me
And a way for you.
And one for Johnny
And one for Sue.
But you can't go back
And you walk alone,
For every Jack
Has a way of his own.

Now, your way is through the garden where the trial is held.

ALICE. How can I get there?

RABBIT. You can't.

ALICE. You're very confusing, I'm sure. First, you say I must go through it—and then you say I can't.

RABBIT. I didn't say that. I said you couldn't go *to* it.

ALICE. Then how am I to go through it? Answer that!

RABBIT. When you belong in the garden it will come to you.

ALICE. I never saw a garden move.

RABBIT. You never saw much and that's a fact. Oh, my whiskers! The Duchess! The Duchess! *(The RABBIT leaps off, watch in hand. ALICE races after him.)*

ALICE. Wait! Please! Rabbit! White Rabbit! Wait, I tell you!

(As ALICE disappears, a CATERPILLAR enters, pushing a mushroom ahead of him. It may be in three dimensions, or merely a cutout. It is large enough for him to lean on or to climb onto, which he presently does.)

CATERPILLAR. What a rumpus! Can I never find a place for a quiet smoke?

(The RABBIT re-enters, U, in great haste. ALICE's VOICE continues offstage, at first pleading, then preemptory.)

ALICE *(offstage)*. Rabbit! R-a-a-bbit! Ra-a-a-a-ab-bit!

CATERPILLAR. Someone's calling you. Can't you make her keep still? It puts me out of sorts.

RABBIT. You talk to her, won't you? I can't wait.

CATERPILLAR. What about?

RABBIT. About her garden. Tell her it will never come to her till she learns to keep her temper.

ALICE *(offstage, in fury). Rabbit! You!*

CATERPILLAR. Such a temper! It makes me feel contrary. You'd better wait and tell her yourself!

RABBIT. It would make me late. I promised the Duchess to speak a piece at her party. I'm to speak, "How Doth the Little." *(The RABBIT poses and speaks with elocutionary airs and graces, his white-gloved hands folded over his stomach, his white-spatted feet turned at a precise angle.)*

How doth the little busy bee
Improve each shining hour,
And gather honey all the day
From every fragrant flower.

Beautiful, isn't it?

CATERPILLAR. If you like it. It makes me feel contrary.

ALICE *(offstage)*. You, Rabbit! White Rabbit!

RABBIT *(scurrying off)*. You tell her about her temper. *(The RABBIT leaves the stage.)*

CATERPILLAR *(calling after him)*. I will if she makes me feel friendly. If she makes me feel contrary, I'll *be* contrary. I won't tell her a single thing.

(ALICE enters.)

ALICE. I declare, it's too bad for him, that it is—Oh-h-h ...*(She stops, looking at the CATERPILLAR, curiously.)*

CATERPILLAR. Who are you?

ALICE. I hardly know, sir. At least, I know who I was when I got up this morning, but I think I must have turned into somebody else.

CATERPILLAR. What do you mean? Explain yourself.

ALICE. I can't explain myself, sir, because I'm not myself, you see.

CATERPILLAR. I don't see.

ALICE. Well, when I got up this morning I was just Alice. But a little while ago I was the size of a rabbit. And now I'm the size of a mushroom. Being so many sizes in a day is confusing.

CATERPILLAR. It isn't.

ALICE. Well, perhaps you haven't found it so yet. But someday you'll turn into a chrysalis, and after that into a butterfly. You'll feel a little queer then, won't you?

CATERPILLAR. Not a bit.

ALICE. Well, it feels queer to me. As if I were somebody stupid.

CATERPILLAR. You are.

ALICE. That I'm not! I'm the head of my class. At least, I was. I'll try if I know the things I used to know. Four times five is twelve—

CATERPILLAR. Wrong.

ALICE. I'll try geography. London is the capital of Paris —That's not right, I'm certain.

CATERPILLAR. Try some poetry.

ALICE. I'll recite "How Doth the Little." *(She folds her hands, clears her throat, and recites, very proud and proper.)*

How doth the little crocodile
Improve his shining tail,
And pour the waters of the Nile
On every fragrant scale.

(She stops, embarrassed, apologetic.) Some of the words have got altered.

CATERPILLAR. It's wrong from beginning to end.

ALICE. You see, sir, I have changed a great deal.

CATERPILLAR. You haven't.

ALICE. Oh, it's no use talking to you! I want to find the garden, where the trial is. The things you say are of no use to me at all.

CATERPILLAR. They are.

ALICE. You make such very short and rude remarks.

CATERPILLAR. I don't.

ALICE. If you're going to contradict every single thing I say—

CATERPILLAR. I'm not.

ALICE. Well, you have been doing, you can't deny that!

CATERPILLAR. I can. *(ALICE stamps her foot, tosses her head, and starts away.)* Come back. I've something important to say. *(ALICE comes back, after a struggle with herself.)* Keep your temper.

ALICE. Is that all?

CATERPILLAR. No! *(He climbs down and pushes his mushroom offstage.)*

ALICE. What else, sir?

CATERPILLAR. Saying it is one thing and doing it another.

ALICE. Keeping my temper, you mean. Well, I'll do my best, sir. I'm usually very polite. But things are so queer down here. What shall I do next?

CATERPILLAR. Ask the Duchess. Knock on her door.

ALICE. There isn't any door.

CATERPILLAR *(disappearing offstage)*. There is.

ALICE. Well! That's not very civil of him!

(As ALICE flounces to C, she stops to stare at the DUCHESS' house, which has entered during the last speeches. At the door stands a FOOTMAN with the face of a FROG. ALICE smoothes out her apron and her hair, speaking softly to herself.)

ALICE. That must be the Duchess' house—now, I'll keep my temper. No matter what happens, I'll keep my temper. *(ALICE approaches timidly, and as the FROG pays no attention to her, she knocks. The FROG is still staring up and ahead.)*

FROG. There's no sort of use in knocking. I'm on the same side of the door as you are.

ALICE. Please, then, how am I to get in?

FROG. Are you to get in at all? That's the first question.

ALICE *(holding her temper with an effort)*. I'd like to ask the Duchess the way to the garden. *(There is a sneezing within.)*

FROG. They're making such a noise in there, nobody'd hear you.

ALICE. But what am I to do?

FROG. Anything you like.

ALICE *(losing her temper)*. There's no use talking to you! I'll just go in myself, that I will!

(ALICE jerks the door open, and a large plate comes skimming out, followed by a pillow. Within is terrific sneezing. The COOK strides out, a pot of soup in one hand and a huge pepper-pot, which she is shaking in all directions, in the other. The FROG sneezes with every move of her arm. ALICE sneezes frantically.)

ALICE. There's certainly—too much—pepper—in that soup!

COOK. Too much? Too *little!* Taste! *(The COOK thrusts a spoonful at ALICE, who emits a perfect volley of sneezes as a result.)*

(The DUCHESS storms out, singing over all the sneezing, which is added to by the baby she carries and spanks in rhythm.)

DUCHESS *(in a singsong voice)*.

Speak roughly to your little boy,
And beat him when he sneezes;
He only does it to annoy,
Because he knows it teases.

Be quiet, pig!

ALICE. You shouldn't call your baby names.

DUCHESS. If everybody minded his own business the world would go 'round a lot faster than it does.

I speak severely to my boy,
I beat him when he sneezes.
For he can thoroughly enjoy
The pepper when he pleases.

(The COOK begins throwing vegetables out of her pot at the DUCHESS, who is quite unconcerned when they hit her and the baby.)

ALICE. Please! Mind what you're doing!

DUCHESS *(tossing ALICE the baby)*. Here...you may nurse it if you like. I've got to get ready to play croquet with the Queen in the garden. *(She turns at the door.)* Bring in the soup. The house will be going any minute! *(As the DUCHESS speaks, the house starts moving. The COOK snatches up her pot and dashes into the house.)*

COOK *(to the FROG)*. Tidy up, and catch us! *(The FROG leaps about, picking up the vegetables, plate, etc.)*

ALICE *(as the FROG works)*. She said "in the garden." Will you please tell me—

FROG. There's no sort of use asking me. I'm not in the mood to talk about gardens.

ALICE. I must ask someone. What sort of people live around here?

FROG. To the right, lives a Hatter. To the left, lives a March Hare. Visit either you like. They're both mad.

ALICE. I don't want to go among mad people!

FROG. You can't help it. We're all mad here. *(He leaps away, but turns back.)* Give me the pig!

ALICE. You shouldn't call the baby "pig."

FROG. That's all you know. *(The FROG shakes the hood off the baby's face, disclosing a little pig, ears, snout, and all. He leaps away, the pig's face over his shoulder.)*

ALICE. Which shall I visit, I wonder? I hope they're not quite raving mad.

(The MARCH HARE hurries in. ALICE backs away, watching anxiously.)

HARE. Here's a place, clean as clean. Not a single crumb.

(The HATTER is appearing.)

HATTER. Help me with the table. *(The HARE and HATTER run offstage.)*

ALICE. They didn't seem to see me. I'm going to be polite this time, no matter what they say. Becaust I must find out how to get into the garden. Because, of course, The Rabbit was talking nonsense. A garden couldn't come to me.

(The HARE and the HATTER enter with the table. During the following they bring in five chairs: one armchair for the head of the table, three small ones for the side, facing the audience, and one for the foot. The movements are so timed that all the speeches are said onstage.)

HARE. Did you tell the Dormouse to bring the chairs?

HATTER. I couldn't find him.

HARE. He's asleep. I put him in the teapot.

HATTER. Then we'll have to carry him, teapot and all—or push him.

HARE. Be quick, or the tea will get cold.

HATTER. You'll have to help me with him.

(The HARE and HATTER bring in the teapot, large enough to hold the actor. It can be made from a small barrel. They have much trouble getting the DORMOUSE

out. Their poking doesn't wake him at first; then he lifts a sleepy head out of the depths, stretches, and settles to sleep again. They take him together, but just as they get him drawn up to his full limp height, he slips down. He hangs over the side. The HARE lifts his arms. The HATTER leans into the pot to get his feet when he falls over the HATTER's back, pinning him into the teapot, etc. At last they get him out and lift or drag him into his seat at the table, all the time sound asleep. They pour the tea, the HATTER pouring and the HARE holding the cups. The tea is in a small container in the spout. They sit on either side of the DORMOUSE, resting their elbows on him and stirring their tea. ALICE approaches timidly.)

ALICE. If you please, will you tell me—

HARE and HATTER. No room! No room!

ALICE. There's plenty of room! *(She sits in the armchair. The HARE and HATTER stare down at her.)*

HARE *(politely)*. Have some candy.

ALICE *(looking up eagerly)*. I don't see any.

HARE. There isn't any.

ALICE. Then it wasn't very civil of you to offer it!

HARE. It wasn't very civil of you to sit down here without being invited! *(The HARE and HATTER stare at ALICE.)*

ALICE. I didn't know it was your table. It's laid for a great many more than three. *(The HARE and HATTER stare at ALICE, saying nothing. Then they drink their tea.)* If you please, will you tell me—

HATTER. Shall we tell her?

ALICE. You don't know what I'm going to ask yet.

HARE. It doesn't matter what it is.

HATTER. What matters is how you behave.

HARE *(nudging the HATTER)*. Ask her a riddle.

HATTER *(to ALICE)*. Why is a raven like a writing desk?

ALICE. I think I can guess that one! *(The HARE and the HATTER look at each other, set down their teacups, and then look at each other again.)*

HATTER. Do you mean you think you can find out the answer to it?

ALICE. Exactly so.

HATTER. Then you should say what you mean.

ALICE. I do. At least, I mean what I say. That's the same thing, you know.

HATTER. Not the same thing a bit. You might just as well say, "I see what I eat" is the same as "I eat what I see."

HARE. You might just as well say, "I like what I get" is the same as "I get what I like."

DORMOUSE *(sleepily)*. You might just as well say that, "I breathe when I sleep" is the same as "I sleep when I breathe."

HATTER. Have you guessed the riddle yet?

ALICE. "Why is a raven like a writing desk?" No. I give up. What's the answer?

HATTER. I haven't the slightest idea.

HARE. Nor I.

ALICE. Well! I should think you might find something better to do with your time than asking riddles that haven't any answers!

HARE *(taking out his watch)*. There's nothing to do with our time but have tea. It's always six o'clock, here.

ALICE. Is that the reason so many tea-things are put out?

HARE. Yes, that's it. It's always tea-time, and we've not time to wash the things between whiles.

ALICE. Then you keep moving 'round, I suppose?

HATTER. Exactly so. I want a clean cup now. *(He calls.)* All move, one place!

HARE *(shaking the DORMOUSE)*. Wake up! Wake up! We want to move.

HATTER. Pour some hot tea on his nose. *(The HARE and HATTER do so, to no avail.)*

HARE. It's no use. He won't wake up till half after six.

HATTER. It's very trying to have a watch always at six o'clock.

HARE. I *told* you to put some butter in it.

ALICE. Oh, please, don't do that!

HATTER. Why not?

ALICE. You'll spoil it!

HARE. It's the best butter.

ALICE. Oh, you mustn't!

HATTER. Did you ever try it?

ALICE. No...

HATTER. Then you shouldn't talk! Hand me the bread knife.

ALICE. Anyway, don't put it in with the bread knife! You're bound to get crumbs in it as well.

HATTER *(brightening up)*. Maybe that's just what it needs.

ALICE. You'll stop your watch!

HATTER. How can I stop it when it isn't going?

HARE. Answer that!

ALICE. I can't, but—

HATTER. Then hold your tongue. *(He puts the butter in with the bread knife, listens to the watch, shakes his head, and looks at the HARE accusingly.)*

HARE. It was the best butter, you know.

HATTER. Try some hot tea. *(The HATTER runs over and dips the watch in the teapot. The HATTER shakes the watch, listens to it, and puts it down, discouraged. The HARE tries it, to no avail.)*

HARE. It's no use. It's still six o'clock. He won't wake up. We'll have to move him. *(The HARE and HATTER have difficulties with the DORMOUSE again. They all move to a clean place but ALICE, who is left with the HARE's.)*

ALICE. This isn't very tidy. It's been used before.

HARE. What's good enough for us is good enough for you.

ALICE. If it was good enough, why didn't you stay there?

HATTER. The rule is: Move down three places.

ALICE. But now that there are four of us—

HATTER. If you can't be civil, you'd better wait till you're invited. *(The HARE and HATTER watch ALICE. She finally sits down, after a struggle with herself.)*

ALICE. It was very nice of you to take me in, I'm sure.

HARE. I vote the young lady recites a poem.

ALICE. I'm afraid I wouldn't get it quite right.

HARE. Recite:

Twinkle, twinkle, little star,
How I wonder what you are.

DORMOUSE *(singing)*. Twinkle, twinkle—

HARE. Pinch him.

HATTER *(doing it, then bowing to ALICE)*. Begin.

DORMOUSE. Twinkle, twinkle, twinkle, twinkle—

HATTER. You pinch him. He doesn't mind me. *(The HARE pinches the DORMOUSE. The DORMOUSE falls asleep.)* Now, then, recite.

ALICE *(reciting).*

Twinkle, twinkle, little bat,
How I wonder what you're at!

I'm afraid that's not quite right.

HARE. There's nothing right about it.

DORMOUSE. Twinkle, twinkle, twinkle—

HATTER. Pinch him on both sides at once. *(The HARE and HATTER upset the milk jug in doing this. It can be so placed that it doesn't show that there is no milk in it.)*

ALICE. Oh! You've spilled the milk.

HATTER. Pick it up, at once!

ALICE. I can't pick up milk!

HATTER. You can't do much and that's a fact. *(The HARE and the HATTER watch her. ALICE keeps her temper with an effort. She points to the floor, above the table.)*

ALICE. I'd be glad to wipe it up, if I had a cloth. It's gone onto the ground, too.

HATTER. There's plenty of clean ground. Help us move the table.

HARE. And mind what you think about while you do it.

ALICE *(helping).* Please, what must I think about?

HARE. All manner of things. Everything that begins with an "M."

HATTER. Mousetraps! The moon! Memory! Muchness!

ALICE. Why with an "M"?

BOTH. Why not?

HARE. Take some more tea.

ALICE. I've had nothing yet. So I can't take more.

HATTER. You mean you can't take less. It's very easy to take more than nothing.

ALICE. Nobody asked your opinion! Or, that is, thank you very much. You're quite right. Of course it's easy to take more than nothing. *(The HARE and the HATTER nod to each other.)*

HATTER. Sit down and do it, then.

DORMOUSE. Twinkle, twinkle—

HARE. Put him in the teapot. *(The HARE and the HATTER go to work at this.)*

ALICE. If you please, and excuse me, O Dormouse, O Hatter, O March Hare, will you be so very good as to tell me the way to the garden?

HATTER. Just keep on the way you're going now. *(He bows.)*

ALICE *(returning his bow)*. Thank you.

DORMOUSE *(standing up in the teapot to bow)*. Good-bye.

ALICE *(returning it, elaborately)*. Good-bye, O Dormouse, O Hatter, good-bye. Good-bye, O kind March Hare.

(The ANIMALS and the HATTER bow themselves and their props off, with increasing ceremony, and ALICE curtsies more and more beautifully to each in turn as long as they are in sight. Positions are such that she does not see bits of the garden which enter behind her from the time she begins to curtsey. If the rocks are to be used for the MOCK TURTLE and the GRYPHON in Act Two, they come on now. ALICE is left alone.)

ALICE. Keep on going, the way I'm going now! But I'm not going anywhere. I'm staying right in one place.

(The RABBIT enters during the last bow.)

RABBIT. The question is: Is there any such thing?

ALICE. Of course there is. Every place is one place.

RABBIT. Certainly not. For instance, this was the place where you lost your temper, wasn't it?

ALICE *(contritely)*. I'm afraid so.

RABBIT. That's one. And now it's the place where you kept it, isn't it?

ALICE. I tried to.

RABBIT. That's two. And it's the place where there wasn't any garden, isn't it?

ALICE. And yet I *did* keep my temper. I was *very* polite.

RABBIT *(as the last piece of garden moves into place)*. That's three. And now it's the place where there *is* a garden. That's four! *(The RABBIT fans himself, faster. ALICE looks around, and cries out in delight.)*

ALICE. What a lovely garden! But I don't see any place for a trial.

RABBIT. How do you know you don't?

ALICE. There ought to be jury boxes where a trial is. I don't exactly know what they are, but I've read about them in the paper.

RABBIT. You don't belong in the trial yet. When you do, the jury boxes will be right here.

ALICE. Will they come when I don't know it, like the garden?

RABBIT. Yes, but you'll have to run very fast. Very, very fast!

ALICE. Why must I run, if the trial is right here?

RABBIT. It'll be one of those times. You have to run as fast as you can to stay where you are. Or faster.

ALICE *(annoyed)*. I wish you wouldn't keep talking nonsense! *(The garden begins to move away.)*

RABBIT. Of course, if you're going to begin losing your temper again—

ALICE *(hurriedly)*. I'm sorry. I'm really very, very sorry. *(The garden returns.)* I can't seem to help it. All the creatures contradict me so. They seem to think I don't amount to anything at all.

RABBIT. The question is: Do you?

ALICE. I'm afraid I don't amount to much. The creatures all find fault with me. They look down on me. It upsets me.

RABBIT. That's *because* you're afraid you don't amount to much. You'll never belong in the trial till you get over that.

ALICE. Oh, Rabbit, can you tell me how I can stop feeling like that?

RABBIT. I can, yes. But it's of no use whatever to tell you.

ALICE. Why not?

RABBIT. You'll never know until you've done it.

ALICE. It sounds sort of easy—just not to let them make me feel good-for-nothing.

RABBIT *(fanning)*. That's it!

ALICE. I'm hoping to find someone and begin! I can hardly wait! *(ALICE cocks her head to listen to the MOCK TURTLE approaching from offstage. The MOCK TURTLE either sings or indulges in chanted lines. Lewis Carroll wrote the lines to "The Evening Star." This may be available in library collections, in a volume, "Good Old Songs We Used to Sing," published by Oliver Ditson & Company. If this song is not available, let the actor chant the lines with great emotion.)*

MOCK TURTLE *(offstage)*.

Beautiful Soup, so rich and green,
Waiting in the hot tureen!
Who for such dainties would not stoop?

Soup of the evening,
Beautiful Soup!

Soup of the evening, beautiful Soup!
Soup of the evening, beautiful Soup!
Beau-ootiful Soo-oup!
Beau-ootiful Soo-oo-oup!
Soo-oup of the e-e-evening!
Beautiful, *beautiful* Soup!

ALICE. Who's that?

RABBIT. It's the Mock Turtle.

ALICE. I never saw a Mock Turtle. What's he like?

RABBIT. He's the one they make mock turtle soup of, of course.

ALICE *(starting, then stopping)*. I feel a little afraid. I suppose it's because I'm not used to him.

RABBIT. You should be glad of that. The thing to be afraid of is getting used to things. Something you never saw before is exciting.

ALICE. Come, now, that's so! I haven't the least idea what a Mock Turtle is, but I won't let him upset me, that I won't! *(She skips gaily toward the exit, but stops suddenly.)* What if I don't amount to much, after all?

RABBIT. Of course you don't. Nobody does.

ALICE. Don't you?

RABBIT. Of course I do. Everybody does.

ALICE. It's very confusing. How can I amount to much and not amount to much at the same time?

RABBIT. That's what nobody knows! But you do.

ALICE. Well, anyway, I'm sure I amount to as much as that Mock Turtle, because he doesn't sing at all well. And I was chosen to sing on the last day of school. It'll be easy not to let *him* make me feel as if I didn't amount to anything! I declare, he's coming here. I'll go by myself and practice. I must begin at once! *(ALICE runs off, waving a hand at the RABBIT, as the song grows fainter.)*

RABBIT *(looking after ALICE)*. That'll never work! The way not to feel good-for-nothing is to forget all about it. And the way to forget all about it is to remember somebody else. Now I wonder whether she'll come across anyone who makes her forget all about it. Well, it won't make any difference in the taste of carrots! *(He takes a huge carrot out of his pocket and nibbles at it ecstatically, his whole body quivering with delight.)*

CURTAIN

ACT TWO

AT RISE OF CURTAIN: *Still in the garden. The MOCK TURTLE and the GRYPHON are seated,C, like the picture in the book (or, if desired, to avoid making the rocks, the GRYPHON may be seated on the ground and the TURTLE pacing up and down). The TURTLE is singing and sobbing, with increasing sorrow, the same song as used in Act One. ALICE enters, full of confidence, tossing her hair off her face, eager for the conquest she is sure of. The TURTLE's sobs arrest her attention. She approaches softly.*

ALICE. What is his sorrow?

GRYPHON. He hasn't got any sorrow. It's all his fancy, that.

ALICE. What a curious creature.

TURTLE *(lifting a scornful head)*. What curious manners. But I don't suppose you've had many lessons in manners.

ALICE. Manners aren't taught in lessons.

GRYPHON. That's all you know about it!

TURTLE *(very superior)*. It's the very first lesson we had in school. The master was an old turtle. We called him "Tortoise."

ALICE. Why did you call him "Tortoise" when he wasn't one?

TURTLE. We called him "Tortoise" because he taught us. Really, you are very dull.

ALICE *(crestfallen)*. What else had you to learn beside manners?

TURTLE. The different branches of arithmetic. Ambition, distraction, uglification, and derision.

ALICE. How many hours a day had you to do lessons?

GRYPHON. Ten hours the first day, nine the second, eight the third, and so on.

ALICE. What a curious plan!

GRYPHON *(disdainfully)*. That's why they're called lessons. Because they lessen from day to day.

TURTLE. Anyone might know that!

ALICE *(trying not to feel put down)*. Well, how did you manage the eleventh day?

TURTLE. We danced the lobster quadrille.

ALICE. I never heard of lobster quadrille.

TURTLE. I don't suppose she could dance it with us.

ALICE *(eagerly)*. I think I could, if you'll show me the steps. I took a prize in dancing class a week ago Saturday. Let's begin. *(The TURTLE and the GRYPHON begin dancing around ALICE, solemnly at first, to their own singing [or reciting, whichever preferred]. The tempo increases as they proceed. ALICE tries in vain to catch the step. They crowd her, bump her, step on her toes, and finally whirl her from one to the other until she goes onto her knees with dizziness.)*

TURTLE and GRYPHON.

"Will you walk a little faster," said a whiting to a snail.
"There's a porpoise close behind us, and he's treading on my tail.

See how eagerly the lobsters and the turtles all
advance!
They are waiting on the shingle—will you come and
join the dance?
Will you, won't you, will you, won't you, won't you
join the dance?"

GRYPHON. There's no use going on with her. She doesn't know anything at all! *(The TURTLE and GRYPHON change the chorus, mocking at ALICE, as they go off, still dancing.)*

TURTLE and GRYPHON.

"Would not, could not, would not, could not, could
not join the dance.
Would not, could not, would not, could not, *could*
not join the dance."

(ALICE springs to her feet in fury as they disappear.)

ALICE. You stepped on my toes and got in my way, that you did! I wouldn't learn the lobster quadrille for anything in the world!

(The RABBIT, who was hurrying by, stops fanning to watch.)

RABBIT. Did you say "wouldn't," or "couldn't"?

ALICE. I said "wouldn't," but I'm afraid I meant "couldn't."

RABBIT *(shaking his head)*. I thought you did.

(The RABBIT hurries offstage. ALICE sinks to the ground, sobbing in despair. From the opposite sides, TWEEDLEDUM and TWEEDLEDEE run on and meet in an ecstatic hug. A sob from ALICE catches their attention. They look at her, once, and then again, turning

their heads together, without breaking their embrace. They speak softly.)

TWEEDLEDUM. Nohow.

TWEEDLEDEE. Contrariwise. *(ALICE looks up. TWEEDLEDUM and TWEEDLEDEE watch her, immovable, standing sidewise as she circles them curiously.)*

TWEEDLEDUM *(as ALICE stops, staring at them, greatly intrigued)*. If you think we're waxworks, you ought to pay, you know.

TWEEDLEDEE. If you think we're alive, you ought to speak.

ALICE. I'm very sorry if I was rude, I'm sure.

TWEEDLEDUM. I know what you're thinking, but it isn't so. Nohow.

TWEEDLEDEE. Contrariwise, if it was so, it might be; and if it were so, it would be, but as it isn't, it ain't. That's logic.

ALICE. I was thinking that I know who you are. *(She points to TWEEDLEDUM, then TWEEDLEDEE.)* Tweedledum! Tweedledee!

TWEEDLEDUM. You've begun wrong. The first thing in a visit is to say, "How d'ye do" and shake hands. *(TWEEDLEDEE and TWEEDLEDUM hug each other and each hold out his free hand to ALICE. She hesitates about which to take first, and finally takes hold of both at once. The next thing she knows they are circling around, singing, "Here we go 'round the mulberry bush." She grows more and more pleased as she dances gracefully and correctly. She curtsies to them gaily as the dance ends.)*

ALICE. You see, I can dance, when it's a sensible dance.

TWEEDLEDUM. Did you think you couldn't?

ALICE. Well, things are so queer, lately. Everything I try to do is wrong.

TWEEDLEDUM. What sort of things?

ALICE. Well, poetry.

TWEEDLEDUM and TWEEDLEDEE *(entranced)*. Do you like poetry?

ALICE. Some poetry. When I know what it means.

TWEEDLEDEE. That *sounds* clever! *(TWEEDLEDUM and TWEEDLEDEE hug each other.)*

TWEEDLEDUM. The trouble is, not everything that *sounds* clever *is* clever. Nohow.

TWEEDLEDEE. Contrariwise.

TWEEDLEDUM. We must find out. *Is* she stupid, or does she only seem stupid?

TWEEDLEDEE. We'll try her on a poem. What shall we recite?

TWEEDLEDUM. "The Walrus and the Carpenter" is the longest.

TWEEDLEDEE. And it has illustrations!

ALICE. Is it sort of an examination?

TWEEDLEDEE. To see whether you are clever or stupid.

ALICE. Oh, dear!

TWEEDLEDUM. Do you like illustrations?

ALICE. Oh, yes! The pictures are the best part of the book!

TWEEDLEDUM. Look behind you. *(ALICE turns to confront a large picture of "The Walrus and the Carpenter," which has come on while they talked. If the group has no one able to copy or draw it freehand, it can be traced from the Tenniel illustration, enlarged on squares, and painted any colors desired. See the Production Notes at the back of the book.)*

ALICE. Oh! What's it about?

TWEEDLEDUM *(springing to one side of it)*. "The Walrus—

TWEEDLEDEE *(springing to the other)*. —and the Carpenter."

TWEEDLEDUM. They were walking together on the seashore and they got very hungry.

TWEEDLEDEE. And they remembered the oysters who lived in the sea.

TWEEDLEDUM. Now, comes the first part of the examination.

TWEEDLEDEE. We'll recite the poem.

TWEEDLEDUM. If you're clever, you can tell when we come to the picture.

TWEEDLEDEE. If you're stupid, you can't.

TWEEDLEDUM. Nohow.

TWEEDLEDEE. Contrariwise.

ALICE. Well, begin.

TWEEDLEDUM *(reciting)*.

"O Oysters, come and walk with us!"
The Walrus did beseech.
"A pleasant walk, a pleasant talk,
Along the briny beach:
We cannot do with more than four,
To give a hand to each."

ALICE. You haven't come to the picture yet.

TWEEDLEDUM. Nohow!

TWEEDLEDEE. Contrariwise! *(TWEEDLEDEE and TWEEDLEDUM hug delighted.)*

Then four young Oysters hurried up,
All eager for the treat:
Their coats were brushed, their faces washed,
Their shoes were clean and neat—

And this was odd, because, you know,
They hadn't any feet.

ALICE *(pointing, excitedly)*. The shoes are here! But you haven't come to it yet because there are more than four.

TWEEDLEDUM. Nohow!

TWEEDLEDEE. Contrariwise! *(TWEEDLEDEE and TWEEDLEDUM hug, more delighted.)*

TWEEDLEDUM.

Four other Oysters followed them,
And yet another four;
And thick and fast they came at last,
And more, and more, and more—
All hopping through the frothy waves,
And scrambling to the shore.

ALICE. I think you must be nearly there. I'm going to listen very carefully. *(She turns her back to the picture, watching the two BROTHERS and listening intently.)*

TWEEDLEDEE.

The Walrus and the Carpenter
Walked on a mile or so,
And then they rested on a rock
Conveniently low.
And all the little Oysters stood
And waited in a row.

ALICE. What were they waiting for? *(TWEEDLEDUM and TWEEDLEDEE watch ALICE, cross-eyed, shaking their heads sadly and speaking softly.)*

TWEEDLEDUM. Nohow.

TWEEDLEDEE. Contrariwise.

ALICE. They must have been waiting for something, you know. *(TWEEDLEDUM fetches a great sigh, and TWEEDLEDEE follows. ALICE looks from one to the other anxiously.)* Don't you feel well? *(TWEEDLEDUM and TWEEDLEDEE turn and look at the picture, sadly. ALICE follows their glance.)* That's it! That's it! You've come to the picture! *(TWEEDLEDUM and TWEEDLEDEE leap up with joy. ALICE hugs each in turn; then they hug each other. BOTH shake hands. They hold out a hand each to ALICE, and the THREE merge into the dance, "Here we go 'round the mulberry bush," as before.)* I passed the first part! Please go on. I can hardly wait for the second.

TWEEDLEDUM. This is just a little clever, you know. Now, we must see whether you can repeat one of the stanzas correctly.

TWEEDLEDEE. If you're clever, you can.

TWEEDLEDUM. If you're stupid, you can't.

ALICE. Oh, dear.

TWEEDLEDEE. Try if you can repeat this.

TWEEDLEDUM. It's the most important part of the whole poem.

TWEEDLEDEE.

"The time has come," the Walrus said,
"To talk of many things:
Of shoes and ships and sealing-wax—
Of cabbages and kings.
And why the sea is boiling hot,
And whether pigs have wings."

TWEEDLEDUM. Now. Repeat it.

ALICE *(dubiously)*. I'll do my best. *(She clears her throat and folds her hands. The TWEEDLES do so, too. ALICE feels for the words at the beginning, but she ends with a burst. The TWEEDLES' lips move with ALICE's throughout.)*

"The time has come"—the Walrus—said,

"To—talk of many things:
Of—uh—shoes—and—ships—and—sealing-wax—
Of cabbages—and kings!
And—why the sea is boiling hot,
And whether pigs have wings."

That's right! I did it! *(TWEEDLEDEE and TWEEDLEDUM hug and hold out their free hands.)*

TWEEDLEDUM and TWEEDLEDEE. Shake! *(They ALL go into the mulberry dance.)*

ALICE. I don't think I was ever so happy in my life! I think I'm going to pass!

TWEEDLEDUM. That's only middling clever, you know. Now, we must see if you can make up your mind.

TWEEDLEDEE. *That* will be very clever, indeed!

ALICE. What must I make up my mind about?

TWEEDLEDUM. Which you like better. The Walrus—

TWEEDLEDEE. —or the Carpenter.

ALICE. Come! That ought to be easy!

TWEEDLEDUM. Nohow!

TWEEDLEDEE. Contrariwise!

ALICE. Well, tell me what each one did. Then I'll know.

TWEEDLEDUM. You must guess what they did from what they said.

ALICE. Go on!

TWEEDLEDEE.

"A loaf of bread," the Walrus said,
"Is what we chiefly need:
Pepper and vinegar besides
Are very good indeed—
Now, if you're ready, Oysters dear,
We can begin to feed."

ALICE. Wait a minute! It sounds to me—they couldn't be so mean! What are they going to eat?

TWEEDLEDUM. What *do* you eat with vinegar and pepper?

ALICE. Oysters! I hate that Walrus! What did the Carpenter say?

TWEEDLEDEE. You'll hear in a minute. He isn't through with the Walrus, yet.

TWEEDLEDUM.

"It was so kind of you to come,
And you are very nice."
The Carpenter said nothing but
"Cut us another slice!
I wish you were not quite so deaf!
I've had to ask you twice!"

ALICE. Then he ate them, too! I hate them both!

TWEEDLEDUM. But you must choose, you know. Listen to the rest.

TWEEDLEDEE.

"I weep for you," the Walrus said.
"I deeply sympathize."
With sobs and tears he sorted out
Those of the largest size,
Holding his pocket handkerchief
Before his streaming eyes.

TWEEDLEDUM.

"Oh, Oysters," said the Carpenter,
"You've had a pleasant run.
Shall we be trotting home again?"
But answer came there none.
And this was scarcely odd, because
They'd eaten every one.

TWEEDLEDEE. Now make up your mind.

TWEEDLEDUM. Which do you like better?

ALICE. That's very hard. I think I like the Walrus better because he was a little sorry for the poor Oysters.

TWEEDLEDEE. He ate more than the Carpenter, though. You see, he held his handkerchief in front so the Carpenter couldn't see how many he took.

ALICE. That was mean! Then I like the Carpenter better if he didn't eat as many as the Walrus.

TWEEDLEDUM. But he ate as many as he could get. And he wanted more.

ALICE. Then I don't like him at all.

TWEEDLEDEE. You must choose, you know, if you're not stupid.

ALICE. It's a puzzler, and that's a fact. How can I like one better when I don't like either of them at all? They're both very unpleasant characters. *(TWEEDLEDEE and TWEEDLEDUM watch her, cross-eyed, very sad.)*

TWEEDLEDUM. I'm afraid she can't make up her mind.

ALICE. I can so!

TWEEDLEDEE *(eagerly)*. Which do you like better?

ALICE *(triumphant)*. Neither one! You can't like anyone better when you don't like him at all! Well, I don't like the Walrus and I don't like the Carpenter, so I don't like either of them better! It's a foolish question!

TWEEDLEDUM *(hugging, ecstatically)*. She can make up her mind!

TWEEDLEDEE *(increasing the hug)*. She's not a stupid child! *(TWEEDLEDUM and TWEEDLEDEE both hold out their free hands.)* She's very clever indeed! *Shake! (They start into the mulberry dance, but are interrupted by a half a dozen or so huge croquet balls, which roll swiftly at their feet. ALICE jumps over one or two as they come.)*

ALICE. Oh-h-h-h!
TWEEDLEDUM. It's the Queen's croquet game.
RED QUEEN *(offstage)*. Off with his head!

(The HATTER rushes in with the very sleepy DORMOUSE, holding him by the nape of the neck, like a kitten, though the DORMOUSE's feet are on the floor as they run. The HATTER hands ALICE his mallet, which may be a flamingo, as in the book, or merely some grotesque-sized mallet.)

HATTER *(to ALICE)*. Here! Hold my mallet while I set up this arch. *(ALICE takes the mallet and watches curiously while the HATTER tries to make the DORMOUSE stand on all fours, for an arch. The DORMOUSE slumps down just as he takes aim with his ball, etc. Meantime, the COOK slides in with a huge tray of tarts, and begins secretively stuffing herself with them. She turns her back, part of the time, turning her head to make sure she is not watched as she stuffs one after another into her mouth. There is a tumult of quarreling VOICES, offstage.)*
RED QUEEN *(offstage, above the tumult)*. Off with his head! Off with your head! On with the game!

(The FROG-FOOTMAN and the CATERPILLAR hurry in, and make two consecutive arches of themselves, and the DUCHESS follows and strikes her ball through them. The RABBIT bounds in, striking his ball after the DUCHESS'. The COOK turns around, her tray entirely empty. She wipes her lips and sighs with repletion.)

ALICE. Were they good? *(The COOK hurls the tray at ALICE and hastily snatches the mallet from the DUCHESS. ALICE dodges the tray, unperturbed, and nods at the RABBIT, triumphantly.)*

(The RED QUEEN [who is the Queen of Hearts] enters, followed by the WHITE QUEEN, the KING OF HEARTS, the KNAVE OF HEARTS [dressed like playing cards], the MARCH HARE, the MOCK TURTLE, and the GRYPHON. ALL are still quarreling, vociferously, the RED QUEEN's VOICE above them all. At sight of ALICE, ALL stop, motionless, the RED QUEEN's arm outstretched, pointing at her. TWEEDLEDUM and TWEEDLEDEE, at one side, arms around each other, watch with anxious sympathy. The RABBIT, the only one to move as all eyes are on her, fans himself, his head on one side, watching ALICE. She tosses her head, self-confident.)

RED QUEEN. Who are you?

ALICE. My name is Alice, so please your Majesty.

RED QUEEN *(shouting at the top of her voice)*. Can you play croquet?

ALICE *(topping her)*. Yes! *(She nods again at the RABBIT, shaking her hair off her face with a little toss of her head.)* See? *(The KNAVE bows deeply to ALICE and lifts a hand to the OTHERS, who break into a song, to the tune, "Bonnie Dundee.")*

OTHERS *(singing)*.

To the Wonderland world
It was Alice who said,
"I've a mallet in hand,
I've a ball on my head.

Let the Wonderland creatures,
Whoever they be,
Come and play with the Red Queen,
The White Queen, and me."

(Chorus.) Then set up the wickets as fast as you can,
And sprinkle the players with buttons and bran.
Put cats in the coffee and mice in the tea,
And welcome our Alice with thirty-times-three.

"Oh, Wonderland creatures,"
Quoth Alice, "draw near.
'Tis an honor to see me,
A favor to hear.
'Tis a privilege high
A croquet game to see,
Along with the Red Queen,
The White Queen, and me."

(The chorus is repeated. ALICE is highly flattered with this, and at the last chorus breaks into a dance, curtsying to one and another during it. Of course, this may be omitted, if desired. She can merely bow elaborately.)

ALICE. You're all very kind, I'm sure. But if I am to play with Queens—

RED and WHITE QUEEN *(in unison, one on each side of ALICE)*. Speak when you're spoken to!

ALICE *(taken aback)*. But if everyone obeyed that rule, and if you only spoke when you were spoken to, and if the other person always waited for you to begin, nobody would ever say anything.

RED QUEEN *(sharply)*. What did you mean by, "if I'm to play with *Queens*"?

WHITE QUEEN *(severely)*. You can't play with us, you know, until you've passed the proper examination.

ALL *(threateningly)*. What did you mean?

ALICE. I only said "if."

RED QUEEN. She says she only said "if"!

WHITE QUEEN. And she said a great deal more than that!

ALL. A great deal more!

ALICE. I'm sure I didn't mean—

KING. You should have meant! What do you suppose is the use of a child without any meaning?

RED QUEEN. Even a joke has some meaning. And a child is more important than a joke.

ALL. I hope!

WHITE QUEEN. You couldn't deny that if you tried with both hands.

ALICE. I don't deny things with my hands!

ALL. Nobody said you did!

RED QUEEN *(suddenly)*. Can you do addition?

ALICE. Of course I can.

RED QUEEN. What's one and one and one and one and one and one and one and one and one and one? *(ALICE covers her eyes, concentrating. ALL the others keep count on their fingers, holding them up at the end.)*

ALICE. I don't know. I lost count.

ALL *(in a monotone)*. She can't do addition!

RED QUEEN. Can you do subtraction? Take nine from eight.

ALICE. Nine from eight? You can't, you know. But—

ALL *(in a higher key)*. She can't do subtraction!

RED QUEEN. Try again. Take a bone from a dog. What remains.

ALICE. Well, the bone wouldn't remain, of course, if I took it. And the dog wouldn't remain. It would come to bite me. And I'm sure I shouldn't remain. I think nothing would remain.

ALL. Wrong!

RED QUEEN. The dog's temper would remain.

ALICE. I don't see—

ALL. She doesn't see!

RED QUEEN. The dog would lose his temper, wouldn't he?

ALICE. I suppose so.

RED QUEEN. Then if he went away, his temper would remain. *Wouldn't it?*

ALL. She can't do sums a bit!

ALICE. I can so, if they're proper sums. *(No one notices ALICE's protest.)*

CATERPILLAR. Recite, "You are old, Father William."

ALICE. I don't know that. But I can recite part of "The Walrus and—"

CATERPILLAR. Repeat it after me. *(He recites with elocutionary fervor.)*

"You are old, Father William," the young man cried.
"The hair which is left you is grey.
Yet you're strong, Father William, a hearty old man.
Now, tell me the reason, I pray."

ALICE. I think I can remember that!

ALL. Don't interrupt!

CATERPILLAR.

"In the days of my youth," Father William replied.
"I remembered that youth would fly fast,
And abused not my health and my vigor at first,

That I never might need them at last."

Now, repeat the whole.

ALICE. I believe I can! *(She folds her hands and clears her throat. TWEEDLEDEE and TWEEDLEDUM do so with ALICE, and follow her words with their lips. At first they show great distress when ALICE goes wrong.)*

"You are old, Father William," the young man said.
"And your hair has become very white.
And yet you incessantly stand on your head—
Do you think, at your age, that is right?"

Some of the words have got altered.

CATERPILLAR. Try the second stanza.

ALICE *(struggling for composure).*

"In my youth," Father William replied to his son,
'I feared it might injure the brain;
But now that I'm perfectly sure I have none,
I do it again and again."

CATERPILLAR. That's not said right.

ALICE *(very low in her mind).* Not quite right, I'm afraid.

RED QUEEN. It's wrong from beginning to end!

FROG *(with a hop toward ALICE).* How tall did you say you were?

ALICE. I'm four feet and—

ALL. Wrong!

FROG. She never said a word like that!

ALL. St-st-st-st-st—

ALICE. I thought you meant: How tall are you?

FROG. If I'd meant that, I'd have said that! There's glory for you!

ALL. There's glory!

ALICE. I don't see what you mean by glory.

FROG. I mean, there's a nice knock-down argument for you.

ALICE. But glory doesn't mean a nice knock-down argument.

FROG *(passionately)*. When I use a word it means just what I choose it to mean. Neither more nor less!

ALICE. The question is whether you can make a word mean so many different things.

FROG. The question is—which is to be master! You or your words! That's all!

ALL (furiously). That's all!

ALICE *(almost in tears)*. Well, anyway, I don't believe—

ALL *(shocked)*. She doesn't believe!

WHITE QUEEN. *I'll* give you something to believe! I'm just one hundred and one years old, five months, and a day.

ALICE. I *can't* believe that!

RED QUEEN. Try again. Draw a long breath and shut your eyes. *(ALICE does so with all her might. EVERYONE else does so, too. As ALICE lets go her long breath, they do, too, and nod to each other, "Yes." ALICE shakes her head, "No.")*

ALICE. It's no use. I *can't* believe impossible things.

ALL *(in low, ominous tones)*. She can't believe!

WHITE QUEEN *(contemptuously)*. I dare say, she hasn't had much practice. When I was her age I always did it for a half hour each day. Sometimes I believed as many as six impossible things before breakfast.

HATTER *(suspiciously)*. Did you say you could play croquet?

ALICE *(hopelessly)*. Well, I used to be very good at it.

HATTER. Let's see you hit the stake!

RED QUEEN. I give you three strokes. Hit—or off with your head!

ALICE. I don't see any stake. *(The HATTER sets the DORMOUSE up on two feet, with considerable difficulty, but finally he remains awake and upright. The HARE puts a mallet into ALICE's hand.)*

HATTER. There.

ALL. Play! *(The KNAVE picks up the empty tray the COOK flung at ALICE, and on it brings her the balls. She takes careful aim, glancing nervously around at the OTHERS, who follow all her movements without taking their eyes off her, leaning down as she does, etc. She straightens up.)*

ALICE. I wish you wouldn't all keep looking at me. *(They ALL look away until she bends down to aim again, when they repeat the performance, every eye intent on ALICE. TWEEDLEDUM and TWEEDLEDEE are in sympathy with her; the OTHERS are not. She finally hits the ball. It is a good shot, but the DORMOUSE jumps into the air so that the ball passes under his feet.)*

DORMOUSE *(as he jumps)*. Twinkle, twinkle, twinkle!

ALL. Missed!

RED QUEEN. One!

ALICE. He jumped up!

RED QUEEN. On with the game! *(The whole thing is repeated, except that they crowd closer this time as ALICE aims. They ALL bend down and watch. The DORMOUSE jumps higher than before, and the cry of the WATCHERS is louder.)*

DORMOUSE. Twinkle, twinkle, twinkle!

ALL. *Missed!*

RED QUEEN. Two!

ALICE *(in tears)*. It isn't a bit fair.

RED QUEEN. *On with the game! (ALICE tries. Again they crowd close, and the DORMOUSE jumps higher than ever.)*

DORMOUSE. Twinkle, twinkle, twinkle, twinkle!

ALL. Missed!

RED QUEEN. Three! Off with her head! *(ALICE throws down her mallet and covers her face in despair. The KNAVE comes to her, his tray still holding balls.)*

KNAVE *(softly)*. The King will pardon you as soon as she's out of sight. He always does.

RED QUEEN *(coming to him)*. What was it you said?

KNAVE. It was of no consequence, Your Majesty. No consequence at all. *(The RED QUEEN stands staring at the tray. She lifts one ball and then another, examining under them.)*

RED QUEEN. Where are the tarts?

KNAVE. Tarts?

RED QUEEN. He stole my tarts! Off with his head! *Off with his head!* Executioner!

(The EXECUTIONER comes on in haste.)

RED QUEEN. Off with his head! At once!

ALICE. No, no, your Majesty.

RED QUEEN. Silence!

ALICE. It wasn't the Knave, your Majesty.

COOK. Who are you?

ALL. *Who are you?*

ALICE *(to the EXECUTIONER)*. You can't take off his head till he's had a trial.

ALL. Who says so?

ALICE. *I say* so. *(A trumpet sounds, offstage.)*

TWEEDLEDUM and TWEEDLEDEE *(together)*. The trial's beginning!

RED QUEEN *(snatching ALICE's hand)*. Run! Run! Run! *(They run faster and faster, without progress, as they are running in place.)*

ALL *(running in place, furiously)*. Run!

RABBIT. So she did it! *(The RABBIT loses ground at this, but recovers with a leap, fanning as he runs. Their bodies bend lower and lower, and their legs go faster and faster, but after the first wild dash to position, no one moves ahead.)*

CURTAIN

ACT THREE

SCENE: *There are two chairs for the KING and QUEEN, and on either side of them are boxes which serve as seats for the jury. The jury is composed of the DORMOUSE, the CATERPILLAR, the HARE, the GRYPHON, the TURTLE, and the FROG. Others may be added, if desired. At the end of one row of boxes is the teapot. At the other end is the mushroom. On each lies a slate and pencil. A platform on which the chairs stand, with steps leading up to them, will be attractive, but is not necessary. In fact, even the jury boxes can be omitted. The jury can sit cross-legged on the floor, bringing in their slates. If jury boxes are not used, all references to them in the lines should be eliminated.*

AT RISE OF CURTAIN: *The RABBIT stands near the thrones, in his herald's dress and holding his trumpet, as in the Tenniel illustrations. ALICE and the RED QUEEN are still running, hand in hand. The RABBIT blows his trumpet.*

RED QUEEN *(stopping)*. We did it! We did it!

ALICE *(gasping for breath)*. Did what?

RED QUEEN. Stayed where we were, till time for the trial. That's speed!

ALICE. It looks like the very same garden we were in when we started to run!

RABBIT. You'd have to run at least twice as fast as you can to get anywhere else. It takes everything you've got to keep the clock from turning back.

ALICE. How strange.

RABBIT. It happens every day, only you don't notice it.

RED QUEEN. They're going to be late. Come and help them along.

ALICE. If you please, I'd like to rest a little. *(The RED QUEEN rushes offstage.)* I think the trial has really come here. Those look like seats for the judges. And those must be for the jury. I suppose that's why they talk about the jury box in the paper. Only, there seem to be a great many of them here. But everything else seems to be just as it was. I declare, I think it's too bad to have to run like that just to stay where you are.

RABBIT. It's worse to go backward, you know.

ALICE. Do you think the Knave really stole the tarts?

RABBIT. What's your opinion?

ALICE. Well, I haven't any yet, because I'm not sure it was the Queen's tarts I saw someone else eat. It would be easier to have an opinion if I knew what I was talking about.

RABBIT. You're wrong about that. The less you know the faster you get opinions.

ALICE. Anyway, the Queen hasn't any right to say, "Off with his head," like that, without a real trial. Suppose the Knave didn't do it?

RABBIT. That would be all the better, wouldn't it?

ALICE. Of course it would be all the better that he didn't do it. But it wouldn't be all the better, his being punished.

RABBIT. You're wrong about that. Were you ever punished?

ALICE. Only when I'd done what I shouldn't.

RABBIT. And you were all the better for it, I know.

ALICE. Yes, but then I *had* done the thing I was punished for.

RABBIT. But if you hadn't done it, it would have been better still, wouldn't it?

ALICE *(puzzled)*. I suppose so. Just the same, if they punish the poor Knave without making sure that it wasn't the Cook, I can't stand it.

RABBIT. When a thing happens, you stand it whether you can or not.

ALICE. Then I won't let it happen, that I won't!

RABBIT. Oh, my whiskers! Here they come.!

(The RABBIT leaps to the thrones and blows his trumpet. The ANIMALS enter first, running furiously, and go to the jury boxes, the DORMOUSE making a dive into the teapot, the CATERPILLAR mounting the mushroom. Each picks up a slate and pencil and begins writing diligently, the pencils squeaking loudly. The EXECUTIONER, TWEEDLEDUM and TWEEDLEDEE, the HATTER, the DUCHESS, the COOK, and the WHITE QUEEN now enter and take places on the sides. Then the KING and RED QUEEN tear in and flop into their seats, assuming sudden dignity. The KNAVE leaps and kneels at their feet. The RABBIT is on one side of the thrones and ALICE on the other.)

RED QUEEN. You are all late. Off with your heads!

ALICE *(gently)*. You were late yourself, Your Majesty.

RED QUEEN. We don't mention that.

ALICE *(leaning over the JURORS)*. What are you writing?

HARE. We're writing down our names, for fear we should forget them before the trial is over.

RABBIT. Order in the court!

KING. Herald, read the accusation.

RABBIT *(reading from a scroll)*.

"The Queen of Hearts, she made some tarts,
All on a summer day:
The Knave of Hearts, he stole those tarts,
And took them quite away."

KING. Consider your verdict.

ALICE. Not yet! There is a great deal to come before that!

ALL *(threateningly)*. What?

ALICE *(unabashed)*. Well, witnesses. *(They ALL subside, looking at each other sheepishly.)*

KING *(meekly)*. Call the first witness.

RABBIT. The Cook! *(The COOK comes forward.)*

KING. Were you in the kitchen when the Queen made the tarts?

COOK. I was.

KING. You saw her make the tarts?

COOK. I oversaw her, Your Majesty.

KING. Was there anyone else in the kitchen?

COOK. Yes.

KING. Woman or man?

COOK. Man. *(The JURORS write it down with much excitement.)*

KING. Describe his costume.

COOK. Can't. Didn't see him.

RABBIT. That's because she didn't look where he was, Your Majesty.

KING. Where was he?

COOK. He was hiding, under tables or behind doors, or in ovens or flour barrels, or things.

KING. Then how did you know he was there?

COOK. Heard him.

KING. What did you hear?

COOK. He sneezed.

KING *(excitedly)*. Try the prisoner with the pepper! *(The COOK does, with many flourishes of the pepper-pot. The KNAVE sneezes loud and long. The OTHER MEN suppress their sneezes, in great anxiety for themselves. KING, with great satisfaction:)* The prisoner was in the kitchen. Write it down.

ALICE. That's not proven, Your Majesty! You should try the other men, too.

ALL. Quiet!

ALICE. It's not fair! *(The RABBIT blows his trumpet.)*

RABBIT. Order in the court!

KING. The Cook may stand down.

COOK. Shan't.

RED QUEEN. Off with her head!

COOK. I can't go any lower. I'm on the floor as it is.

KING *(graciously)*. Then you may stand aside. Call the prisoner.

RABBIT *(after blowing his trumpet)*. The Knave of Hearts. *(The KNAVE comes forward, trembling, his face quivering with fear.)*

Smile in the presence of the King—
I said smile, not smirkle.
Mouth a semicircle!

KING. That's the proper style. *(The KNAVE smiles.)* Jurors! Listen closely. I'm about to make a searching test. Prisoner, do you know how tarts are made?

KNAVE *(brightening)*. I can answer that! You take some flour—

COOK. Where do you pick the flour? In the garden or the window boxes?

KNAVE. It isn't picked. It's ground.

WHITE QUEEN. How many acres of ground? You mustn't leave out so many things.

ALICE. Flour for tarts isn't measured in acres. It's measured in cups—or quarts or barrels. The Cook is spelling it wrong.

KING. It's of no consequence. It's plain he knows how to make tarts. That proves he was hiding under tables or in barrels, watching the Queen at her cooking. Write it down.

ALICE. It proves nothing of the sort! *(The whole COURT turns on ALICE.)* Well, anyway, I don't think it does.

CATERPILLAR. You. Who are you? *(The DORMOUSE cheers.)*

RABBIT. Suppress the applause! *(The EXECUTIONER puts the cover on the teapot. The DORMOUSE shortly lifts it off again. The HATTER springs forward wildly.)*

HATTER. Hold that evidence! *(There is excitement in the court.)*

KING. Have you fresh evidence? *(The HATTER stares at something unseen in intense excitement, and then passes through surprise into deep dejection.)*

HATTER. No—I—

I thought I saw an elephant
Playing on a fife.
I looked again and saw it was
A letter from my wife.
At length I realize, O King,
The bitterness of life.

KING. That's the most important bit of evidence we've had yet. It practically proves the prisoner guilty. Let the jury consider it carefully.

ALICE. If any of them can explain it, I'll give him a sixpence. I don't believe there's an atom of meaning in it.

KING. If there's no meaning in it, that saves a world of trouble, you know, as we needn't try to find any.

ALICE. But then you can't call it evidence against the poor Knave.

FROG. It's very provoking to be told we can't call a thing evidence we wish to call evidence! I call anything evidence I wish to do! *(He wags a finger at ALICE and speaks with sepulchral mystery.)* Impenetrability. That's what I say.

ALL *(imitating the FROG's action and tone)*. Impenetrability.

ALICE. Will you please tell me what "im-pen-trability" means?

FROG. By impenetrability I meant, just now, "We've had enough of that subject and it would be just as well if you would hold your tongue as I don't suppose you mean to stop here all the rest of your life interfering with this trial!" So! *(The FROG is on his feet, shaking his fist at ALICE at the end of his speech, and the OTHERS imitate him.)*

ALL. So!

ALICE *(calmly)*. I shall interfere with this trial just as long as it isn't fair. So. *(ALICE smiles. The OTHERS subside, exchanging shame-faced glances and hanging their heads. The RABBIT blows his trumpet softly. TWEEDLEDUM and TWEEDLEDEE hug each other.)*

RABBIT. Your Majesty must cross-examine the prisoner.

KING *(with an uneasy glance at ALICE)*. Well, if I must, I must. Where were you when the tarts were set out to cool?

KNAVE. In the garden.

KING. Did you see anyone there?

KNAVE. I saw the Cook.

COOK. Nothing of the sort! Ask him if he spoke with anyone!

KING. Did you speak with anyone?

DUCHESS. He spoke with me!

KING. Did he show any signs of having eaten tarts?

DUCHESS. He's eaten a great many.

KING. How do you know?

DUCHESS *(bridling)*. He paid me compliments.

KNAVE. I deny that!

DUCHESS.

You haven't forgot the identical spot
Where you stopped me from singing a ditty.
When you *said* I was plain and excessively vain,
But I knew that you meant I was pretty.

KNAVE *(in despair)*. I didn't know I meant that!

COOK. He's too afraid of being found out to know what he means!

KING. I fear he ate the tarts. I fear he ate them all! Write it down.

ALICE. Stuff and nonsense! What sort of evidence is that? Rub it out! *(The JURY does so hastily. The RABBIT fans himself daintily. TWEEDLEDUM and TWEEDLEDEE hug each other.)*

RABBIT. Your Majesty must cross-examine the ditty sung by the Cook.

KING *(with great dignity)*. Call the Ditty.

RABBIT *(blowing his trumpet)*. The Ditty! *(EVERYONE leans forward. The DUCHESS holds her hands over her stomach and sings rapidly, but each word is very clear. The tune is "Yankee Doodle," repeating the music for the third line three times.)*

DUCHESS *(singing)*.

There was a pig who sat alone,
Beside a ruined pump.

(The JURY, who writes furiously throughout her song, sings the last syllable, and makes a noisy period on their slates with a great flourish.)

JURY *(singing)*.

Pump.

DUCHESS *(singing)*.

By day and night he made his moan—
It would have turned a heart of stone
To see him wring his hooves and groan,
Because he could not jump.

JURY *(singing)*.

Jump.

DUCHESS *(singing)*.

Up rose that pig and jumped full whack
Against that ruined pump.

JURY *(singing)*.

Pump.

DUCHESS *(singing)*.

He first saw red and then saw black,
And rolled right over on his back;
His snout caved in, his bones went crack.
It was a fatal *j-u-u-u-m-p*.

JURY *(singing)*.

Jump!

KING. And the prisoner spoke about the ditty, when you had finished?

DUCHESS. At the top of his voice!

KING. And he didn't know what he meant! That looks very bad. *(They ALL nod. The HATTER gives a shriek, and rushes to C, pointing at some unseen thing over which he drops his hat with great cavorting.)*

HATTER. Ha-a-a-ah! *(The RABBIT sounds his trumpet loudly. The KING rises and cries even louder than the HATTER.)*

KING. Evidence!

RABBIT. The Mad Hatter! *(The HATTER lifts his hat cautiously, and then feels under it with growing surprise and disappointment. He rises and backs away, his finger still pointing, full of mystery and dread.)*

HATTER.

I thought I saw a rattlesnake
That questioned me in Greek
I looked again and saw it was

(He speaks in a hushed tone.)

The middle of next week.
The one thing I regret, O King,
Is that it cannot speak.

(The KNAVE shrinks away from the spot the HATTER's finger points at, his eyes full of fear. His hand clutches his throat.)

KNAVE *(in a terrified whisper)*. The middle of next week—

GRYPHON. He looks guilty.

HARE. He acts guilty.

FROG. He is guilty!

TURTLE *(with a sob)*. We are ready with the verdict. *(The DORMOUSE cheers.)*

WHITE QUEEN. Suppress that Dormouse! *(The DORMOUSE dives down in the teapot himself. He pops out again as soon as the TURTLE sings.)*

TURTLE. Shall we say it, or sing it?

ALICE. You couldn't possibly be ready to give it yet?

RABBIT. Sing it.

TURTLE *(To the tune of "Solomon Levi")*.

I'll tell thee everything I can:
There's little to relate.
I saw an aged, aged man
A-sitting on a gate.
"Who are you, aged man," I said,
"And how is it you live?"
His answer trickled through my head
Like water through a sieve.

And now, if e'er by chance I put
My fingers into glue,
Or madly squeeze a right-hand foot
Into a left-hand shoe,
Or if I drop upon my toe
A very heavy weight,
I weep, for it reminds me so
Of that old man I used to know

(Repeat line of music.)

That summer evening, long ago,
A-sitting on a gate.

ALICE. You certainly can't call that a verdict!

FROG. I can and I do!

ALICE. It's just nonsense!

RED QUEEN. You may call it nonsense if you like, but *I've* heard nonsense compared to which that would be as sensible as a dictionary.

RABBIT. The question is: "Is a dictionary ever sensible?"

KING. Consider the verdict.

ALICE. There's nothing in that song to consider.

TURTLE *(loftily)*. I hadn't come to the verdict. That must be whispered. *(The DORMOUSE runs to the TURTLE and, standing on its toes, receives the whispered verdict with squeaks and growing excitement. It then runs to the HATTER and delivers it into his ear, with more squeaks and excitement. The HATTER removes his hat and crosses solemnly to the KING, leaning close to his ear. He stands up again to hand his hat to one of the JURORS, and cups both hands over the KING's ear. He shouts at the top of his voice into it.)*

HATTER. *Our verdict is—(EVERYONE jumps. The KING leaps to his feet.)*

KING *(furiously)*. Do you call that a whisper? *(The HATTER swiftly gets back to his place. The KING speaks with recovered dignity.)* If you do such a thing again, I'll have you buttered. *(ALICE giggles.)* Silence. *(He puts a hand to his head and thinks intently.)* Rule Forty-Two. Any child who laughs out loud must leave the court.

ALICE. That's not a regular rule. You invented it, just now.

KING. It's the oldest rule in the book.

ALICE. Then it ought to be Number One!

KING *(hastily)*. On with the execution.

ALICE *(between the KNAVE and the EXECUTIONER)*. You can't do that! The idea of having the execution first! You haven't even had a sensible trial yet!

KING. First the execution, then the verdict, then the trial.

ALICE. Nothing of the sort.

COOK. Anyway, we *have* had a trial.

ALICE. You haven't called all the witnesses. *I* have some evidence to give.

COOK *(in great haste)*. Your Majesty, here is something that was picked up in the garden. A scroll. *(She hands the KING a scroll.)*

KING. What's in it?

COOK. It seems to be a letter written by the prisoner.

KING. Who is it directed to?

COOK. It isn't directed at all. That's the strange part of it.

KING. Is it in the prisoner's handwriting?

COOK. No, it isn't. And that's the queerest thing about it.

KING. He must have imitated someone else's hand.

KNAVE. Please, your Majesty, I didn't write that and they can't prove that I did. My name's not signed at the end.

COOK. There's no name signed at the end.

KING. If you didn't sign it, that only makes matters worse. You must have meant some mischief or you'd have signed your name like an honest man.

COOK. That proves his guilt!

ALICE. It doesn't prove anything of the sort. You don't even know what the letter is about.

KING. Herald, read it. *(The RABBIT takes the scroll and unrolls it. It is five to six feet long, with some rolled scroll at the bottom still. It is backwards, "looking-glass" writing, and there is a murmur of astonishment and suspicion from the COURT.)*

RABBIT. It isn't a letter at all! It's a set of verses.

HATTER. He's disguised his handwriting!

COOK. It's a secret code!

KNAVE. It isn't mine! I couldn't write like that if I tried.

KING. Don't try to pull the wool over my eyes. You've written it so no one but yourself can read it. Very well! Read it yourself. Begin at the beginning and go on till you come to the end.

KNAVE. I can't read it!

KING. Can anyone else read this scroll? No? Then it's plain he wrote it so no one could, on purpose. There's no telling what's in it. This is terrible!

ALICE. You don't know whether it's terrible till you know what it says. Anyway, nobody knows the Knave wrote it.

COOK. Read it yourself, if he didn't write it! Either he wrote it for himself alone or somebody else can read it.

KING. Isn't that true?

ALICE. It sounds true. But there's something wrong about it.

ALL. Read it yourself, then! *(The DORMOUSE cheers.)*

KING. Suppress that Dormouse! Off with his whiskers! Remove him from court. *(Several carry the DORMOUSE out in the teapot, or he himself walks the teapot out.)*

ALICE. It seems to me I have seen writing like that somewhere before. *(They ALL watch ALICE intently, but she doesn't notice them.)* If I could remember where I stood and what I was doing. Yes! I was combing my hair! In front of the looking glass! It's looking-glass writing. All you have to do is to read it backward! The title is "Jabberwocky."

COOK. If she's so sure of that, let her read it, Your Majesty. Let her read without a stop.

KING. I give you one hundred and eighty-two seconds! *(The JURORS begin tapping out the time with their pencils on their slates, and ALL the others join in, each in his own fashion, in keeping the rhythm going. It gets faster and faster. ALICE keeps perfect time with them, going at last at lightning speed, but with every word perfectly clear.)*

ALICE *(reading)*. "Jabberwocky."

'Twas brillig and the slithy toves
Did gyre and gimble in the wabe.
All mimsy were the borogroves,
And the mome raths outgrabe.

"Beware the Jabberwock, my son!
The jaws that bite, the claws that catch!
Beware the Jubjub bird and shun
The fruminous Bandersnatch!"

He took his vorpal sword in hand:
Long time the manxome foe he sought—
So rested he by the Tumtum tree,
And stood awhile in thought.

And, as in uffish thought he stood,
The Jabberwock, with eyes of flame,
Came whiffing through the tulgey wood,
And burbled as it came.

One, two! One, two! And through and through
The vorpal blade went snicker-snack!
He left it dead, and with its head
He went galumphing back.

"And hast thou slain the Jabberwock?
Come to my arms, my beamish boy!

O frabjous day! Callooh! Callay!"
He chortled in his joy.

ALL *(on the last syllable)*. One hundred and eighty-two!

ALICE *(her hand on the KNAVE's head)*. Saved!

RED and WHITE QUEENS *(to the KING)*. How do we know that's what it says?

ALICE. Just turn it around and you can see for yourselves! *(The RABBIT and the other ANIMALS turn it so the light comes through it and it can be read.)* There!

COOK. Hold your tongue!

QUEEN. Off with your head!

KING *(to the EXECUTIONER)*. Off with her head! *(The EXECUTIONER strides to ALICE, axe uplifted, followed by the KING and QUEENS in royal rage. ALICE faces them, unflinchingly.)*

ALICE. Who cares for you? You don't amount to anything. You're nothing but a pack of cards! *(ALICE blows at the EXECUTIONER contemptuously. He is whirled around as if by a high wind. As she chases him, still blowing, he is blown off the stage, together with the KING and QUEENS, who try to interfere and are greeted with gusts from ALICE and go whirling off in different directions. There is a great whirling and scurrying from all the OTHERS as ALICE bounds about, blowing with all her might. The KNAVE whirls offstage in a dance of joy, TWEEDLEDUM and TWEEDLEDEE hug in ecstasy and whirl off with the royal seats; the RABBIT blows his trumpet now and again in delight at ALICE's courage, and all the OTHERS leap and turn and bound away, carrying whatever props they are concerned with. ALICE is left alone on an empty stage, dizzy with her own bendings and turnings, laughing in triumph. She sinks to the ground, her laugh fading. She is asleep.*

From offstage come the VOICES of TWEEDLEDUM and TWEEDLEDEE.)

TWEEDLEDEE *(off)*. She doesn't feel good-for-nothing anymore.

TWEEDLEDUM *(off)*. Nohow.

TWEEDLEDEE *(off)*. Contrariwise. *(The RABBIT's trumpet sounds softly, offstage.)*

TWEEDLEDUM *(in a vanishing voice)*. Nohow.

TWEEDLEDEE *(very faint)*. Contrariwise. *(A vanishing note of the trumpet is heard, very far away. There is silence. If a kitten is available, it comes to ALICE. [One can easily be trained to do so by finding a bit of food under her hand]. If none is used, a kitten's mew comes from offstage. ALICE sits up, rubs her eyes, and looks around in delight.)*

ALICE. The sky! My kitten! *(Either ALICE runs offstage, calling "Kitty, Kitty," or she stands holding the kitten as the curtain falls.)*

CURTAIN

PRODUCTION NOTES

COSTUMES: Costuming of the animals may be carried out successfully on any of three different levels:

1. It may be *suggestive* merely, depending on movement and expression for characterization. In this case there need be no mask and but little attempt to give shape to the body. The RABBIT, DORMOUSE, and MARCH HARE should wear hoods with the proper ears attached and whiskers of proper length on the upper lip. Make-up should be mixed to match the hood at its edge and blended into the foundation used for the face, in order that the line of the hood may not be too marked. Otherwise, the make-up should be used to emphasize characteristic expressions. There should be a flap on the hood, long enough to prevent risk of its pulling out when tucked into the collar. The FROG-FOOTMAN wears a helmet-like cap suggesting the general shape of the head. This may be made of buckram, or even stiff paper if it is to be used for few performances. If the play is to be repeated often, papier-mâché is needed. Movements and postures suggest the character, i.e., the RABBIT's entrances and exits are with a light leap; the FROG holds his arms and legs akimbo and moves by hops, etc. There is a definite advantage in having the face thus free for expressiveness, and the voice not muffled by masks. Children enjoy this costuming quite as much as complete masks.

2. If the production is to be carried out by the children themselves, they will greatly enjoy painting flat masks on stiff paper or buckram and fastening them to hoods. This will mean that the side view is curious, but the scenes can be played largely front-view, and the discrepancies of the side view seem not to trouble a child audience at all.

3. Complete masks may be used. Directions for making them may be found in Dunn's book, "Marionettes, Masks and Shadows," and in Remo Bufano's "Be a Puppet Showman." For amateurs, the gauze or screen-piece in front of the actor's mouth should be as large as possible, and carefully placed, or it will be found to be above or below, when worn. Masks tend to muffle and distort the voice. Experiment will show what pitch and volume of each actor carries best within his particular mask. Large gestures should precede and accompany lines spoken by masked players, as otherwise the audience is slow to know which is speaking.

All the costumes may be taken direct from the Tenniel illustrations, and colored to suit the producer's fancy. Also, the director can be guided by these illustrations in grouping and stage pictures.

SCENERY: There is actually no scenery required. The play is done on a bare stage with drapes or some other neutral background. Change of scene is indicated by the use of moving props.

MOVING SCENERY: Flats or screens with small returns on each side furnish perfectly satisfactory scenery. Corrugated pasteboard covered with furniture wrapping paper makes movable scenery which is inexpensive and easily handled by young actors. The DUCHESS' house, the mushroom, and the garden pieces may be handled in this manner. They may either be put on rollers, rubber-tired, to be had at a hardware store for little, or carried on by unseen actors or stagehands. If rollers are used, the scene should be fastened to a small frame, and extend below it, just missing the floor. Or, they may be flat cutouts with handles for moving and a brace for support. If the scenes are carried in, loose cloth should hang to the floor to hide the movers' feet. This frame may be merely painted, or given contour: a roof with a chimney shape on it for the DUCHESS' house; cutouts of flowers and shrubs for the garden. The DUCHESS' house may be large enough for both the COOK and the DUCHESS. The actors and props may enter behind it, or it may stop near enough to a side wing for them to move behind it, unseen. The actors may come through a practical door, or around from behind the house. In that case, ALICE will pound on the door instead of throwing it open. The pillow and plate can be aimed as the actors come around the house.

THE MUSHROOM: The mushroom may be made simply in two-dimensional form of corrugated paper or wallboard, the CATERPILLAR leaning on it instead of climbing on to it. This is simply painted. Or, it may be a substantial structure mounted on a rolling platform, with invisible steps for the CATERPILLAR to climb up (see diagrams at the end of the "Production Notes"). The latter is made of a substantial frame covered with wire netting and canvas and then painted. In either case, the mushroom is designed with the top tipped back from the audience, so that the silhouette is a wide circle.

THE JURY BOXES: These are merely light boxes, painted and decorated. Although it is indicated that the jury boxes can be eliminated and the jurors can sit cross-legged on the floor, it is far better to use the boxes. A child audience does not like people sitting on the floor, for the simple reason that in many auditoriums they are too hard to see.

THE TEAPOT: The teapot may be made of a small keg or barrel with a handle of wood attached. The spout (of papier-mâché) may have in it a funnel, or bottle, which will hold tea, so that it can actually be poured out. This is very effective, though not necessary. The cover is made of papier-mâché or wire, covered with canvas. The bottom is open so that the DORMOUSE can walk off with it at the end of the scene, bowing between steps. The teapot might be simply a cutout with a lid that comes off. The DORMOUSE can enter behind it. The lid can have decorative projections which slip into slits on the back of the teapot, to hold it in place. If the keg with the actor in it is too heavy for the HATTER and HARE to lift, it can be put on rollers and shoved in, or it can be made with an open bottom, so the DORMOUSE can walk it on. It must then have room for him to do so without showing. The appearance of the DORMOUSE from the teapot is the important thing. Place the teapot in *front* of the table, and to one side, as the children enjoy it too much to have it hidden by the table.

PROPERTY PLOT

ACT ONE:

- Watch (Rabbit)
- Fan (Rabbit)
- Large carrot (Rabbit)
- Mushroom and hookah (Caterpillar)
- *House for* (Duchess:)
  - Pillow and plate to be thrown out.
  - Pot of soup for Cook.
  - Pepper-pot for Cook.
  - Large spoon (Cook)
  - Pig wrapped up as a baby (Duchess). Only the head need be a pig. It may be made of cloth and stuffed,

or made of papier-mâché.
Vegetables (Cook)

Table for tea party:

Five chairs
Teapot with tea in the spout (Dormouse)
Four cups and saucers
Four teaspoons
Watch for Hare
Butter in a dish (Hatter)
Bread knife (Hatter)
Milk pitcher to knock over

Set pieces for garden

ACT TWO:

Rocks, if desired (Mock Turtle and Gryphon)
Picture of "The Walrus and the Carpenter"
Six or more croquet balls [beach balls, painted]
Mallets (Hatter, Duchess, and Rabbit-possibly others)
NOTE: Flamingos, cut from cloth and stuffed, can be used, following the Tenniel drawing. Ordinary mallets of exaggerated size also may be used
Tray of tarts (Cook)

ACT THREE:

Seats (King and Red Queen)
Mushroom and teapot
Boxes, if desired (Jury)
Slates and pencils (Jurors)
Trumpet (Rabbit)
Scroll (Rabbit)
Axe (Executioner)
Hat (Hatter)
Pepper-pot (Cook)

Scroll (Cook)
Kitten, if desired

THE SCROLL: It is necessary to print only one stanza of the "Jabberwocky" poem. Alice takes it and lays it on the floor, rolling it back with her foot as she reads. Except for the first stanza, there need be only black marks, as the lettering will not show. Of course, she has it memorized for lightning speed.

ENLARGING A PICTURE ON SQUARES:

The picture of "The Walrus and the Carpenter" can be enlarged accurately from the Tenniel illustration by using the "square" method. It can be painted in any color. While the accompanying illustrations have been ruled with an uneven number of squares, you will find a division into an *even* number of squares will simplify computation when dividing the larger square to match equally the smaller one.

Take the picture off from the book on tracing paper. Cover it with an even number of small squares. Cover the surface on which you wish to draw the enlargement with an equal number of squares. Since you have an even number of small squares, the size of the large ones can be determined by dividing length and breadth of the surface in half, then dividing that in half again, etc.

Draw the picture so that each line in the enlargement cuts the length or breadth of a large square in the same proportion as the corresponding line in the original picture cuts the small squares—that is, note whether it crosses at 1/2 or 1/3 or 2/3, etc., of the length or breadth of the small square. It is helpful to note the relation of the lines to the corners and the centers of the squares.

When making scenery by this method, one often finds the large squares enormously larger than the original. It is then helpful to measure the large squares accurately into halves, fourths, thirds, etc. All guiding lines should be very faint, so that they may be readily painted over, or erased. It is sometimes useful, when the difference in size is very great, to make an intermediate sketch. Children enjoy doing this enlarging for their own show, from the sixth grade up.

The first drawing shows the mushroom as seen by the audience. The second drawing is a rear view, showing the steps for the Caterpillar to climb up.

The White Rabbit wears white spats and white gloves. The costume for the Dormouse can be made from loose brown cotton flannel. The Frog-Footman wears a green and brown hood, and moves in hops. The Mock Turtle has a brown hood and brown body, with cow horns. The shell is made of heavy paper or papier-mâché. His tail should be long enough to be kicked around. Fasten the shell around the body with straps carried through slits in the suit. For balance, a small slit should be made in the feet of the Caterpillar's costume. He moves on all fours, doubled like an inchworm. His costume is green with green make-up on his face. The Gryphon wears a feathered headdress, and points on the end of his gloves. Any colored suit with a feather effect painted on it would be satisfactory.

Enlarging a Picture on Squares

The smaller drawing indicates the original picture, which is to be enlarged by the "square" method. It has been taken off the book on tracing paper and covered with a number of small squares. The larger drawing shows how the picture is transferred to the enlargement, after which the guide lies are painted over, or erased.